I0408379

All About Hypnosis
A Modern Hypnosis Guide

Dedication:

This book as with all of my books is dedicated to my amazing daughter, who inspires me and drives me to be better every day.

I love you Christy Lee

And of coarse to my wife Karen who stands by me and helps my in all my endeavors. Love ya baby.

Introduction

I want to thank you for learning all about hypnosis and joining me on this journey. Every year I work for thousands of people and educate them about the value of hypnosis.

In this booklet it is my desire to reveal to you how you can take control of your life and achieve your goals with remarkable ease. This book can guide you to higher personal and professional satisfaction.

I know these are strong claims. Coming from a skeptical and scientific background, I hesitate to even suggest such benefits, however the data is irrefutable.

On this page it may be to early for me to tell you this, but your life may never be the same.

You see, you hold in your hands a tool that will allow you to tap into the power of your mind, to control your destiny and enrich your life and the lives of others.

This tool does not take a lot of time, nor is it expensive. It only requires a small investment of your time and willingness to experience its usefulness. Nothing more.

I'll see you on the path.

What is Hypnosis?

Most people are use to the image of hypnosis that is portrayed in the movies and on the television. This is a far cry from the actual state of hypnosis.

Hypnosis is a natural state of mind that each of us experience every single day. Have you ever found yourself engaged by a project that focused all your attention on the task at hand and time seemed to fly by?

Have you ever tried to speak with somebody who was working behind a computer keyboard and you had trouble getting his or her attention? That is a natural state of hypnosis.

Here is a simple definition of hypnosis that most researchers agree on:

"The ability to follow suggestion without conscious intent."

You may be interested to know that in the laboratory setting, researchers have used hypnosis to create false memories, hallucinations and alternative behavior in people so that they could be studied and analyzed.

Let's consider those studies and the recent hypnosis knowledge that has come to light.

Recent Hypnotic Discoveries

Over the last several years there have been significant advances in neuroscience, which has allowed us to more effectively study hypnosis. In fact, science has developed instruments for studying hypnosis. This has allowed hypnosis to come out of the dark ages and enjoy its current mainstream success.

One of the cutting edge tools that is used to study the hypnotic state is called a Positron Emission Tomography (PET) scan. It records an actual image of the brain, during the brains thought process.

It is found that hypnosis produces a very specific pattern of activity within the brain. It shows an increase blood flow in the right anterior cingulate cortex.

Based on the tasks of the right anterior cingulated cortex, this suggests that there is an internal focus. This brain activity is very different from normal and waking states. Let's consider brain wave activities.

There are four types of brain wave classifications.

They are:
• Beta

• Alpha

• Theta

• Delta

Beta waves are the normal waking consciousness state. As you read this book, you are in beta. Beta is a state where you are wide-awake and aware of your surroundings.

Alpha waves are a slower pattern that are found when people relax, listen to music or meditate.

Theta waves are present just before and after you awaken from deep sleep. They are also present during the hypnotized trance state.

Delta waves are deep sleep. Delta allows you to rejuvenate and dream.

Using the PET scan, scientists have made some exciting discoveries regarding hypnosis. For instance, some people have concluded that hypnosis is simply imagination. This is now proven to not be the case. It has been determined there is absolutely no relationship between hypnosis and imagination.

While in a state of hypnosis, many people experience auditory (sounds) and visual hallucinations. This is the reason people often times connect imagination with hypnosis.

Using the PET scan, researchers have discovered different regions of the brain are utilized during hypnosis which differ from the regions of the brain exercised while using imagination.

That means when a person imagines a sound, the activity is located in a different place in the brain. When that same person experiences a hypnotic hallucination, the brain activity is recorded in an entirely different area.

Studies done at McMaster University in Ontario, Canada used a PET Scan to record the brain activity of hypnotized individuals who imagined a scene and then who experienced a hypnotic hallucination scene.

Researchers found that auditory hallucination and imagining a sound are both generated within each of us. However the hallucination in hypnosis, like that of real hearing, is experienced as being received from an outside source.

Researchers then tried to isolate the area of the brain responsible for this different brain response pattern while in hypnosis.

Eight subjects were studied by the University in Ontario, Canada during this amazing session.

During the session, each person heard the exact same audio track while the PET scan recorded the brain activity. The brain activity was studied during four different circumstances:

1) While they were listening in their normal waking state.

2) While they rested and listened to the audio.

3) While they just imagined to hear the audio track.

4) While they were in a hypnotized state responding to suggestion to hallucinate the audio track, although it was not actually playing

The research revealed the region of the brain called the right anterior cingulate cortex was just as active while the volunteers were hallucinating as it was while they were actually hearing the track.

In comparison, the right anterior cingulate cortex was not active at all while the volunteers were imagining they heard the audio. Clearly something tangible is going on!

Hypnosis had completely fooled the right anterior cingulate cortex area of the brain into registering the hallucinated voice as genuine.

Hypnotic Myths

Some people erroneously believe that in order to be hypnotized you must be weak willed. Numerous studies have shown that hypnotizability is completely unrelated to that characteristic. Hypnotizability has nothing to do with gullibility, submissiveness, imagination or being weak willed.

In fact, the stronger your will, the better your concentration, the faster the easier you go into a trance state.

Some people believe that in order to be hypnotized you must put forth effort. Studies have shown this is also incorrect. Most hypnotized people say, "It just happened."

In fact, often times, if people are having trouble experiencing hypnosis it is because they are trying too hard. It's when they relax and try less, hypnosis happens!

Can I Be Hypnotized?

Some people say, "hypnosis sounds wonderful but I don't think I can be hypnotized!" Well, they may be surprised to learn that they already experience hypnosis on a daily basis. Let us look at examples of daily hypnosis.

Have you ever found yourself completely immersed in an activity to the exclusion of everything else? That is a natural trance state.

Common examples of this are:

While watching a movie and becoming transfixed in the plat.

Reading a book and been so transfixed that you did not hear someone come in and speak with you.

Driving down the freeway and experiencing highway hypnosis is not witchcraft, manipulation or magic. It simply is a tool that will allow you to tap into the power of your mind

What is Required to be Hypnotized?

All that is required to be hypnotized is a a willingness and a minimum of an IQ level of 60

How does Hypnosis work?

Hypnotic change works through the power of suggestion. in order to fully understand the how, it's important to discuss the mechanics of your conscious and subconscious state.

Each day we fluctuate between the conscious and subconscious state of mind. Recall the last time you operated your vehicle. Perhaps it was while you were going to work, shopping or to the doctor's office. Think about that trip. Do you recall the details of that drive? I doubt it. Most people do not consciously drive their vehicles.

For most people driving is something done in our unconscious mind. You don't say to yourself, "I must put the vehicle in gear, release the parking brake, check over my shoulder for oncoming traffic, signal to turn left, release the steering wheel to right the vehicle and stay in this lane."

Driving is typically done unconsciously. Your subconscious is aware of everything that is happening but consciously your thinking about things you need to do, thinking of things you want to watch on television later, or things you wished you would have said or done.

We tend to multitask, all day long. We easily and naturally move between the conscious to the subconscious.

Hypnosis allows us to place suggestions directly into the subconscious mind and what takes hold in the subconscious is automatically acted on by the conscious mind.

The Personal Benefits of Hypnosis and Common Hypnotic Applications

What changes would you like to make?

Would you like make changes in your:

1. motivation

2. confidence

3. attitude

4. focus

5. goal orientation

6. stress levels

7. weight

8. smoking habit

With hypnosis you can. In fact, specific behavior change is the most common use of hypnosis.

Most people try to make behavior changes based on self-discipline and will power. The problem is this is an inefficient and ineffective way to facilitate long-term change. Hypnosis is much more effective.

How It Feels To Be Hypnotized

I'm sure you have seen zombie-like characters in the movies and on television who are supposedly in a hypnotic state of mind. This common misconception can create resistance for those who are being hypnotized for the first time.

It can be hard to allow yourself to relax if you think that under hypnosis you surrender all control of your behaviors to the hypnotist.

In fact, when you are hypnotized, you are in more control than when you're in the normal daily state. You become internally focused, and your surrounding environment becomes less important and insignificant.

If for any reason there were an emergency or your attention was needed, you would immediately emerge yourself to respond appropriately.

Emerge means to come to a full waking state.

People in a hypnotized state may appear to be asleep, but the biological state of sleep is very different from hypnosis.

While your body is relaxed, your mind will be fully alert and aware of the suggestions it is receiving. All outside stimulus will become irrelevant. Your focus will be directly on the words of the suggestions you are receiving and your breathing will be light and rhythmic.

You may have a distorted sense of time. You may feel like you have been in hypnosis for just a couple minutes, even if it has been sixty to ninety minutes.

Now that you know what it feels like, it's time to learn....

How to Hypnotize Yourself

Now that you understand the power of the sub-conscious mind and the role that hypnosis can play in reaching and influencing it, the next step is to hypnotize you.

The tools you will use are suggestion, concentration and imagination.

The ability to relax and just let it happen is important. If you try too hard, you will become tense, and that is the opposite of what you are trying to accomplish. If you take a "prove it to me" attitude, you will also impede your progress. Cooperate and you will get your proof.

One reason people have difficulty learning self-hypnosis is that they do not know when they are hypnotized. The very act of questioning requires the use of critical thought and thus breaks the trance state.

The student of self-hypnosis must learn to question after, not during, the hypnotic session. Many times, because they expect something different, people believe they have failed to achieve the trance state, when they have not failed at all.

The light trance, the feeling I just described, is easily obtained with self-hypnosis and is sufficient for reaching the subconscious to plant suggestions. The medium trace naturally follows with practice. The deepest level appears to be, but is not, deep slumber.

Make sure that you avoid an analytical attitude. Analyzing will keep the conscious mind alert, which is self-defeating. If you follow the directions in this chapter and just let it happen, it will.

It is now time for you to experience self-hypnosis. In this booklet we only have the room to cover one technique.

Following the self-hypnosis instruction I will coach you on where, when and how to apply this technique for it's maximum effectiveness.

It is easiest to break down the self-hypnosis process in 5 components:

1) Mindset

2) Induction

3) Deepening

4) Suggestions

5) Awaken

1) Mindset

You must be willing to be hypnotized. Your mindset should support your hypnosis session by focusing on the goal you wish to achieve regardless of whether that is a specific change in your behavior (goal oriented such as weight loss) or just simple relaxation. Consider the goal of your session, the outcome you desire and be expectant of reaching your goal.

2) Induction

The induction is what you will use to turn your focus from external to internal. The induction will allow you to tap into the power of your mind to reach your desired outcome by programming your subconscious. And we know what is programmed on a subconscious level will automatically be adopted by your conscious mind.

Here is how you do it:

First, make a recording of the following script. Make your recording in the second person throughout. It is presented here in the second person, so you may read directly from the book into the microphone.

Begin reading in a soft, relaxed voice. Draw out your voice and pause often between sentences. Your voice and the pace of your speech should suggest drowsiness and relaxation.

After you have recorded the induction and before you record the "wake up" section, you may want to record the suggestions you wish to make. If you prefer, you may leave a blank space on the tape so that you may give yourself mental suggestions.

Next, with the recording made, sit or lie comfortably with your arms parallel to your body. Separate your feet eight to ten inches, so the thighs are not touching. Loosen all tight clothing.

Here is your self-hypnosis induction:

"Take a moment and make yourself comfortable in a sitting or reclining position.

Loosen all tight clothing and prepare to enjoy a few moments of complete and total relaxation.

Let's begin by taking a deep breath all the way in, and as you let it out, just allow your eyes to close.

Another deep breath now, and this time, as you let the breath out, begin to relax your entire body.

As we go through this process known as progressive relaxation, you will find that it will become very easy for you to just relax and let go and allow yourself to drift into the most relaxed and peaceful state of mind you have ever experienced.

Another deep breath, and as you let the breath out, let your thoughts move to your right leg. Begin now to relax all of the muscles in your right leg.

Relax them; allow the muscles to just let go. Imagine a wave of relaxation flowing through your right leg from the sole of your foot... up through your ankle... through your calf, relaxing every muscle, every nerve and every fiber, and up through your thigh now.

Relaxing your hips and every muscle as it flows.

Feel this warm relaxing wave flowing down into your left leg now.

Flowing down into the calf now - relaxing. Flowing on to the very tips of your toes - every muscle every nerve ever fiber so very relaxed.

This wave of relaxation flowing through both of your legs now leaving them so very heavy and relaxed.

The legs so heavy now you don't even want to move them.

Up through your waist relaxing every muscle and every nerve and every fiber.

Feel this wave flowing up now through your back, relaxing every muscle, just letting go.

Your shoulders relax it seems as if some tremendous weight has been lifted from your shoulders.

And this wave of relaxation flows down into your right arm relaxing every muscle nerve and fiber.

Down into your forearm and wrist now. Relaxing even down to the very tips of your fingers.

Now begin to relax the muscles in your left arm from the shoulder down through the forearm and wrist relaxing down to the very tips of your fingers.

Every muscle just letting go.

Both arms so very heavy - you don't even want to move them- both arms like a wet rag now.

And around to your chest.

Become aware of your breathing now.

Breathing easily now, and with every word I speak and every breath you take, you will find it will become easier for you to just relax and let go.

Breathing deeply now... and with each breath relaxing even more.

Feel the warm wave flowing around your shoulders now, releasing all tension.

Feel your body becoming so very heavy now.

This wave of relaxation is flowing up through your neck... relaxing... up into your scalp now... relaxing every muscle and tiny nerve.

The muscles around your eyes are relaxing now. Your eyelids becoming so very heavy.
Today is past.

Tomorrow is a thousand miles away, but right here, right now, there are no worries or cares, only a few moments of complete, total relaxation.

Your eyelids are so very heavy now, it would be too much of an effort to even try to open them, but why try, it feels so very good just to relax....Completely.

The muscles around your jaw and throat are relaxing now.

It feels so good just to relax and let go.

Enjoy this feeling of total relaxation.

All problems are left behind now.'

3) Deepening Your Hypnotic State

In order to deepen your hypnotic trance state you should provide yourself with the following suggestion:

"With each count from five to one, I will drop down twice as deep." "As I descend this staircase (in my mind), I will drop down deeper, with each step I take down I descend to a place of peace and contentment."

Five) letting go of everything
Four) feeling light, distant, relaxed
Three) dropping down deeper than ever before
Two) from here out, with every step down I will drop twice as deep as before. One) All the way down, more relaxed than ever, feeling peaceful and content.

I would recommend that you repeat this deepening process three times. You will start to feel detached. Anyone watching you will notice that your breathing pattern has become light, your heart rate will be altered and your blood pressure has changed. You are in a state of hypnosis.

I would recommend that with every self-hypnosis session you do, you always give yourself the suggestion: "I will drop down deeper and deeper with each session, faster and faster."

You will quickly find yourself dropping down into wonderful and peaceful states of trance quickly.

Initially, you may wonder if you are really hypnotized. This is completely natural. If you are following the instructions on the previous pages, you can rest assured you are hypnotized. In addition, in the coming pages I will teach you how to prove to yourself you are in a hypnotic trance.

Many people wonder how deep they have to be in order to receive the benefits of hypnotic suggestions. Studies show even in light trance depth you will receive the wonderful benefits of hypnosis.

4) Hypnotic Suggestions

Prior to your hypnotic trance you want to form your hypnotic suggestions. Your suggestions should always be phrased in the positive, never in the negative. You should also phrase them in the present, never in the past or future.

Here is a weight loss example suggestion:

Correct Example:
"I weight 180 pounds and find greater satisfaction with smaller portions."

Incorrect Example:
"I'm on my way to losing weight and giving up foods that are bad for me."

In the second example, you will notice it is phrased in the negative, giving up foods and losing weight. In addition, you will notice the incorrect phrase of timing.

Your subconscious mind will hear these suggestions and take them literally. It will think you are on your way, but it's not time yet to lose the weight.

Here is a Stress Control Suggestion:

Correct Example:
"I control my stress level and release those things I cannot control."

Incorrect Example:
"My life will be less stressed when I worry less about those professional and personal worries that are out of my control."

Think about those areas of your life you would like to improve and then work on one specific area during your trance session. Don't work on multiple tasks in the same trance session.

Some people think, "I'll work on stress, pain control and weight loss during the same session." It is too much and you will dilute the value.

Think of the specific goal you would like to achieve. Record that goal. Then start to structure suggestions that will allow you to achieve it. Be positive, be present and be brief.

Edit your suggestions down to simple sentences. In a typical trance session you should use no more than four suggestions that support the single goal you have chosen.

Repetition of each suggestion is important to achieve that desired goal. Repeat each suggestion six to eight times per self-hypnosis session.

5) Awaken

The final step in self-hypnosis is to awaken yourself. You do that by giving yourself the following suggestion: "In a moment I will count from one to five. I will awaken feeling refreshed, energized and looking forward to my next session. Allowing myself now to fully integrate each suggestion I have provided myself which supports my goal.

With every session I will find myself dropping down deeper, faster and enjoying it more and more."

" One, imagining that I'm back at home just like I am every morning; two, allowing the energy to fill my limbs; three, becoming more aware of my surroundings; four,

appreciating the time I spend for myself and the value it provides; five, wide awake and noticing how good I feel."

Congratulations on your trance session. In five steps you have programmed your mind to help you accomplish your goals. Don't under estimate the power of this formula; research has proven its effectiveness!

You can purchase professional hypnotic scrips to read for your self here:

www.hypnosisdownloads.com

I would suggest reading them and then rewriting them in your own words.

How Can I Prove To Myself That I'm Really Hypnotized?

Here is an advanced, little known technique that you can use to confirm you are in a state of hypnosis.

This test should occur after the deepening component and prior to the behavior change suggestions.

1) Give yourself the suggestion that as you relax, your mouth will begin to fill with saliva and as you swallow it, it will take you down deeper.

If your mouth begins to fill with saliva then you know you are hypnotized and responding to suggestion!

or

Give yourself the eye lock test.

It would be recorded like this: " Now draw your attention to those eyes. Relaxing those eyes all the way. Making those eyes to lazy, loose and heavy. So heavy that you couldn't open those eye even if you tried. In just a minute I'm going to have you test those eyes but don't test them until your sure they won't open. Test them now on the count of three 1..2..3.. Great now stop testing and allow that level of relaxation to flow over your entire body."

How Long Should My Trance State Last?

There is no set time requirement for a hypnotic session. It only takes a couple of minutes to enter this state of mind and program yourself for success.

When I'm at home and on my regular schedule, I prefer to do twenty minute hypnotic sessions. If my schedule will not permit this length of time, then I experience a quick five or ten minute session.

Where Should I Experience Trance?

Never experience hypnosis while driving or operating any machinery.

Many people use hypnosis during their normal day activities such as when they are on a break at work, on a bus or airplane.

If you will be using hypnosis at home, I would recommend you experience your trance session seated or reclined in a chair, couch or bed and let your significant other or kids know you are not to be disturbed unless an emergency occurs. This is your time for yourself, enjoy it.

HOW MANY SESSIONS ARE SUGGESTED FOR PERMANENT RE- SULTS?

I recommend you work on one specific change (weight loss, confidence, etc.) for twenty- one days straight. Research shows this is the opportune length of time to achieve your goal and make long term permanent change.

Obviously, before making any changes in your medical or physical well-being, you should consult your physician.

What's On The Immediate Horizon

We are just now beginning to enter a phase where hypnosis will grow exponentially and improve the lives of those who utilize this powerful tool. I believe that with the current research that is possible in neuroscience, and the realization of both individuals and corporations that hypnosis can be extremely valuable, the horizon for hypnosis is brighter then ever.

Hypnotizing Others

Now we as hypnotist have a great re-
sponsibility to use our powers for good.
You have been given a gift now. A gift
that will allow you to share relaxation,
motivation & relieve with the people you
hypnotize.

I would highly recommend you get
some additional study resources found
at the back of this book to increase your
knowledge before you go to crazy. But
here are some basic to get you started.

Step 1: Establish Rapport

What we want to do quickly here is
1)Get their interest sparked
2) gain their confidence
3) Get rid of any fears

4) In general make them comfortable with the idea of being hypnotized by you.

How do we do that. First we let them know we are hypnotist. We state that as a fact. Say it with confidence, "I am a hypnotist." Now you need to act confident about this fact. Don't giggle or act silly as you say this. Don't give them any reason to think you might be joking or play around.

The subjects belief that you can hypnotize them is the number one most important requirement for this process. If they believe you can, then you can.

So on Stage I have a pre-recorded introduction that say : And now ladies and gentlemen give it up for Robert B. The Hypnotist."

In the streets it might go more like this.
Me: "Hey have any of you ever been hypnotized before?"
Response 1: "Yes, ...
Me: Great I'm a hypnotist would you like to relax with some hypnosis now.

.

Or it might go like this

Response 2: "No"
Me : Well today's your luck day. I'm a
hypnotist would you like to see what
hypnosis feels like

Great now we have their interest peaked
or perhaps a conversation started.

Now we are going to gain their confidence. How do we do this? Well one
way is by being the expert. You need to
be the guy or girl with all the answers.
Don't let them rattle your cage with any
question. be ready with an answer. hear
are some stock answers to questions
you might hear, and if they aren't asked
you can alway introduce the question
your self so that you can answer it.
Such as:

"People ask me all the time : Can you
get stuck in hypnosis.:
Answer: No, it's impossible to get stuck
in hypnosis, worst case scenario, you
would just slip into deep sleep only to
awaken refreshed when you were ready.

Question: What is hypnosis
Answer: There are many theories and a lot of people have come up with a lot of different definitions. But this is what we do know, hypnosis is an intense focus on one thing, thought or idea, occupying the conscious mind. We call this trance and while in trance the mind becomes more suggestible and open to ideas.

Question: Doesn't that take a week minded person.
Answer: No the exact opposite is true. The more intelligent you are the better subject you will be.

This pre-talk is going to serve a couple of functions: It is going to help me see who is interested and engaged. It is also going to help me establish my rapport with the Audience. Your audience or subject needs to like and trust you for them to be able to be hypnotized by you. So try to be kind, friendly and generally likable .

Next we are going establishing compliance. This is where we start testing them to see if they are going to be a good subject as well as get them use to taking our directions.

Your going to move them around a bit. "here move your chair a little this way." & "Sit back, feet flat on the floor, each hand resting comfortably on each knee"

Watch your subject make sure they are following along as you start giving them directions. If they resist you at all during this faze they are probably not going to be a good subject and you might want to just do a classic placebo demonstration. Which I 'll explain next.

The finger test is a great next step. Here is how it works. Use the following script while demonstrating the actions along with your subjects.

Script: " Rub your hands together like your trying to warm them up. Now on the next count of three clap your hands together interlocking your fingers and squeeze tight. 1,2,3"

"Your doing great now on the next round of three extend those 2 index fingers straight out about 1 inch apart, then imagine that there are magnets on each of those fingers"

"Imagine that you can feel those magnets pulling those fingers closer and closer until they touch.

"Alright get ready on the sound of three extend those two first fingers 1,2,3."

Now start describing the force of the magnets, " As you listen to the sound of my voice and focus on the tips of your fingers you will find they are coming closer and closer and closer.....etc"

Watch your subjects. This test acts as a convincer and as a test. The fingers coming closer together is a purely physiological occurrence. If the are responding they will be convinced of your power and we are ready to move on. If they are not responding, they are fighting the natural physiological impulse and will probably fight you the whole time it is better to let them go with a " Don't worry about it, you probably just have a lot on your mind" statement, this puts everything on them and makes the next volunteer want to succeed.

Now it's time for your induction. There are a lot of books out there teaching a lot of different inductions. Finding your own induction is up to you. There are instant induction and rapid induction and slow progressive relaxation inductions. You should probably start simple. Start with seated subjects, it is safer and easier.

1   Look into their eyes as if you're looking right through them. If your subject has trouble looking you directly in the eye, you can try having them look at a spot directly underneath one of your eyes.

2   Once their gaze is fixated on you, have them take a couple of deep breaths. As they exhale on the last breath tell them to close their eyes. Tell them to relax their whole body and as you say that cup the back of their head lightly, or simply put one finger on the

back of their head. This slight move will automatically make you the more dominant party and you can continue to direct their attention after that. Next, tip their head forward gently with your hand or finger as you say "sleep." Don't pull or yank their head, just tip it slightly. This is a reflex and it will last only a split second.

3   The moment you say "sleep" you need to deepen the level of trance. You can say something like "That's right, drift ,dream & float, because the more you relax, the better you feel and the better you feel the more you relax. You can also say "deeper, deeper and deeper"

4   Continue to deepen the trance, but make sure your subject is well balanced so they don't fall over. You can easily do this by grasping their shoulders to make them feel more secure.

5   At this point you can proceed
     with your routine, but don't for-
     get your audience. Make sure and
     speak up so you can be heard by
     the crowd. Don't stress out if
     something goes wrong, because
     more than likely it will! If some-
     thing doesn't go right, just laugh
     it off. The goal is to have fun and
     enjoy yourself, because street
     hypnosis is not something to be
     taken too seriously.

6.   Now it's time to waken your partic-
     ipants. Before we do let clean up
     by saying something like, " in just
     a moment I will awaken you and
     when I do everything will be back
     to normal, you will no longer be a
     duck" or what whatever sug-
     gestions you had given. Let us
     also leave them with some posi-
     tive suggestion to thank them for
     their participation.

8   Awaken them using the technique
     taught earlier in this book.

Safety First

Alway remember to think through your suggestions. Your volunteers are placing themselves in your hands. Do not break that trust by having them do any thing dangerous or humiliating.

Always have you participant open their eyes before you have them do any activity that involves them leaving their seat. They will remain in hypnosis even tho their eyes are open if you give them that suggestion.

A Hypnotic abreaction is a emotional outburst or a release of held in emotions. On rare occasions you might have someone act out in a strange or unusual ways. It is best to know what to look for and how to handle it should this happen to you.

If you notice someone shaking, crying, moving or act out out in any unusual way, be on the save side: relax and in a calm relaxing voice bring that person out of hypnosis and thank them for their participation.

The worst possible thing to do is to panic of act worried this plays into the phobia and escalates the problem. Just put one hand on their shoulder and start the awakening

More resources:

For those looking to learn more I would recommend the following reading materials

Anthony Jacquin - Reality is Plastic - 2007

Ormond McGill- The New Encyclopedia

of Stage Hypnotism

These two books will give you a great

start.

Conclusion

I want to thank you for joining me and learning about hypnosis. I encourage you to begin to use this powerful tool to make the changes that will benefit you and create the life you desire.

I'm certain you will find your new life rewarding and exciting.

I wish you much success personally and professionally and hope you will use the power of hypnosis to create a more rewarding future for yourself and your loved ones and I hope to see you soon in my audience.

I look forward to hearing of your success!

Robert Berry

www.Robert-Berry.com

www.TheHypnotist.us

The End